First published in Great Britain 1977 by Ward Lock Ltd.
Copyright © 1977 by Grisewood & Dempsey Ltd.
All rights reserved. a b c d e f g h
This edition is published by Derrydale, a division of
Crown Publishers, Inc.
Printed in Singapore by Tien Wah Press (Pte) Ltd.

Library of Congress Cataloging in Publication Data

Ardley, Neil.
  Let's look at birds.

  Includes index.
  SUMMARY: An introduction to the birds of the world and
their characteristics and behavior. Includes birds of the
tropics, sea and shore, river, marsh, woods, fields, and
town.
  1. Birds--Juvenile literature. [1. Birds]
I. Rignall, John. II. Millington, Richard. III. Allen,
Graham, 1940- IV. Justice, Jennifer L. V. Title.
VI. Title: Birds.
QL676.2.A72 1979   598.2   79-84394
ISBN 0-517-28724-2

LET'S LOOK AT
BIRDS

Written by Neil Ardley

Illustrated by John Rignall,
Richard Millington, and Graham Allen

Edited by Jennifer Justice

DERRYDALE · NEW YORK

What is a Bird?

There are more than 8000 kinds of birds in the world. Some live in hot, steamy jungles; others live in cold lands, on high mountains, or in deep valleys. There are birds of the plains, fields and forests, the seashore and the oceans. Even cities and towns are homes for many different types of wild bird. Each kind, or "species," of bird has its own body shape and a special type of beak and feet.

Birds can do all kinds of things. Most can fly and almost all of them can also walk, hop or run along the ground. Many birds can swim, while some can even dive under the water.

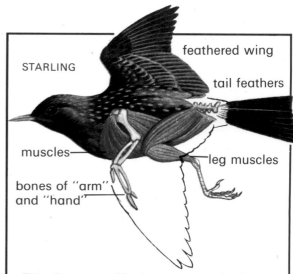

Birds are all shapes and sizes, but most of them have the same parts to their bodies. The wings are like arms, with feathers attached to long "hand" bones.

Flying

A bird does not fly like an aircraft. An aircraft has an engine to move it forward, and wings that raise it in the air when it is moving. A bird flaps its wings to do both these things. The wings push air down to raise the bird, and push air backward to move the bird forward. Birds may also stretch out their wings and glide.

Then it flaps its wings downwards. It holds its wing feathers close together to push air down and back. It tucks its feet up close to its body.

A sparrow, like most land birds, begins its flight by jumping into the air from the ground or from a perch.

sparrow

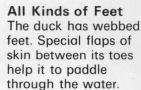

All Kinds of Feet
The duck has webbed feet. Special flaps of skin between its toes help it to paddle through the water.

duck

The eagle has sharp, hooked talons to grip and slash its prey.

eagle

The ostrich has strong, wide feet so that it can run quickly over the grasslands where it lives.

ostrich

The sparrow's wings and tail feathers are fully spread to slow it down just before it lands.

Getting ready to land, the sparrow pushes its feet out towards the branch.

When it raises its wing again, the feathers part to allow the air to pass through the wing.

The largest bird of all is the ostrich. It is 8 feet (2½ meters) tall, much bigger than a person. Its egg is 8 inches (20 cm) long. The smallest bird is the Cuban bee hummingbird. It is only 2½ inches (6 cm) long and its egg is ⅜ inch (8 mm) across.

woodpecker

The woodpecker has two toes pointing forwards and two pointing backwards to help it to grip tree trunks.

finch

Finches have three toes in front and one behind for holding onto perches.

coot

A coot has flaps of skin along the sides of its toes to help it swim.

ostrich

Cuban bee hummingbird

The tiny Cuban bee hummingbird compared in size with an ostrich.

ostrich egg

hummingbird egg

Attracting a Mate

song thrush

gannets

In the spring, a male bird must find a female so that they can mate and have young. The birds usually stay together until the young leave the nest. But some birds stay together all their lives. They may return year after year to the same nest. More often, they build a new nest each year.

A male bird often marks out an area where he will find food, attract a mate, and raise a family. This area is called a territory. The song thrush's territory may be the size of a large garden.

Gannets and other sea birds nest in large groups. Each bird has a territory not much bigger than the size of its nest.

Some bower birds make a "hut" of twigs and grass in their territory. They decorate it with colorful flowers, shells and berries to attract a female.

female bower bird

male bower bird

great crested grebes

Pairs of great crested grebes perform special dances before mating. The actions help the birds to trust each other.

At left, the grebes shake their heads at each other. Then one bird "pops" up in front of the other.

One grebe may lower its head and spread its wings right out over the water in a special pose.

Finally, the two birds dive under the water, and then rise up with weed in their beaks.

A male bird will frighten away any other male from his territory. Some birds will even attack their own reflections, thinking they are rival birds. On the right a male chaffinch attacks his own image reflected in the hub cap of a car. The red breast on the "other" chaffinch tells him it is a male.

Courting

Male birds may show off their feathers in special ways to attract, or court, the females. Courting actions and songs help a pair of birds to trust each other instead of fighting.

The peacock raises his beautiful feathers in a great fan of colored plumes to court the female. The peahen, the female, does not look anything like the male. This is because she must look after the young. If she were as brightly colored as the male, her plumage would attract enemies to the nest.

chaffinch

peahen

peacock

Nests and Young

Early in the breeding season, many birds build nests so that they can safely rear their young. Many birds weave a nest of twigs, grass and feathers among the branches of a tree or bush. Other birds nest on the ground, either among grass or stones or in burrows. Some birds do not build a nest at all. They may lay their eggs on the ground or even bury them under the earth!

The eggs must be kept warm until they hatch. Sometimes the parent birds take turns sitting on the nest to keep them warm. When the chicks hatch, their parents feed them and protect them from enemies. Soon they are big enough to learn to fly and find food.

The tailorbird (1) sews leaves together to make a cup in which to nest. Weaver birds (2) build hanging "baskets." The ovenbird (3) makes an oven-shaped nest of mud. The fairy tern (4) simply lays its egg on a branch.

herring gull

The herring gull has a red patch on its bill. The chicks peck at this patch to make the parent bird give them some food.

young herring gulls

reed warbler

young cuckoo

female mallard duck

ducklings

Not all birds have to feed or even look after their young. Some chicks are born with feathers and can run about or swim soon after they hatch. Ducklings (above) follow their mother at first for protection, but they are able to find food for themselves.

The common cuckoo does not look after its young at all. It lays its egg in the nest of another bird. This bird then looks after the young cuckoo instead of its own chicks.

Migration

Many birds fly great distances to another part of the world for the winter. This kind of journey is called a migration. The birds go to warmer places where they will be able to find food. When spring comes, they fly back again to breed. Often, they come back to exactly the same place every year to nest.

swallow

When winter comes and food is difficult to find, the swallow migrates to warm lands (above). There it will find insects to eat. In the spring, it flies back to its summer home to breed (below).

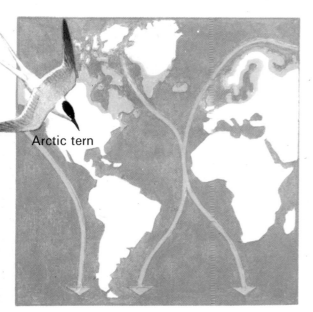

Arctic tern

The Arctic tern (left) migrates farther than any other bird. It flies from the Arctic to the Antarctic. The map shows the routes the terns take.

swallow's nest and young

11

River and Marsh

Streams, lakes and marshes are homes for many different birds. The reeds of a marsh or stream are a perfect hiding place for shy birds such as the bittern and water rail. Their streaky coloring matches the reeds so well that it is difficult to spot them. The shallow water in a marsh and at the edges of lakes and rivers attracts many wading birds. They walk through the shallow water, prodding the mud with their beaks in search of food.

The open water of a lake or river is home to swimming birds. Ducks, geese and swans paddle through the water, lowering their heads beneath the surface to feed. Other birds such as diving ducks and dippers dive right under the water to feed.

dipper

The dipper can dive to the bed of a stream and walk along the bottom. It spreads its wings and heads into the current to stop itself from floating back to the surface.

swallow

A swallow swoops low over the water to catch insects.

Canada geese

Canada geese swim on the water but usually feed on grass on the shore.

cygnets

mute swan

A mute swan glides through the water. It carries its young, called cygnets, on its back when they get too cold and tired to swim.

kingfisher

In a flash, a kingfisher darts from its perch on the bank and plunges into the water to seize a fish in its beak.

A heron prepares to stab at a fish with its long, sharp beak.

heron

bittern

mallard duck

A male mallard duck takes off from the surface of the water. Mallards often live in ponds in city parks.

Sensing danger, a bittern "freezes" with its beak raised so it looks like the reeds behind it.

The water rail is a shy creature. It hides in the reeds, coming out to the shore to look for food.

water rail

A coot keeps a close eye on its young. The coot's nest may be built on plants growing at the water's edge.

coot

young coots

13

blue jay

Woods and Fields

The trees of a forest or wood provide shelter for many birds. Small birds such as finches, thrushes and warblers flutter in and out of the leafy branches. They look for insects or seeds and berries to eat, and places to nest. Woodpeckers live on the tree trunks, pecking insects from the bark and nesting in holes in the wood. Hunting birds such as falcons and owls fly over the tree tops, watching with their sharp eyes for small birds, mice and other prey.

Birds of fields and moors do not have the protection of trees. They live and nest on the ground. Many are protected by their coloring, which hides them from enemies. Some birds can be found in both woods and fields. Starlings sleep in trees but come to fields to feed. Finches leave the woods in search of food in winter when seeds are scarce, but return to the trees to nest in spring.

A blue jay screams at a long-eared owl roosting on a branch. Owls sleep in trees in the daytime, when other woodland birds often try to drive them away. The long "ears" of this owl are in fact just tufts of feathers.

long-eared owl

The nuthatch clings to a tree trunk, using its beak to dig insects from the bark.

treecreeper

nuthatch

The treecreeper walks along the branches, digging for insects with its long, curved beak.

wood warbler

crossbill

The wood warbler flutters from tree to tree in search of insects.

The crossbill tears open a fir cone with its scissor-like beak to eat the seeds inside.

The wood pigeon is a seed eater. It often leaves the woods to feed in fields, where it can be a pest to farmers.

acorn woodpecker

An acorn woodpecker drills a hole in the tree with its beak. It stores acorns in the hole to eat later.

wood pigeon

woodcock

The woodcock hides among the plants and dead leaves on the ground, using its bill to dig for worms.

woodcock

owl

The position of a bird's eyes on its head tells us about its way of life. The owl is a hunting bird. Its eyes are at the front of its head so that it can easily locate its prey. The woodcock lives on the ground. Its eyes are at the sides of its head so that it can keep watch all around and see any enemies before they see it

The skylark flies straight up into the sky when it is disturbed, singing sweetly as it hovers over the field.

skylark

raven

The raven eats the flesh of dead animals, called "carrion." Ravens live in forests and moorland, often building their nests on rocky ledges.

Pheasants live and nest on the ground. The cock, or male pheasant, is brightly colored to attract its mate. The hen, or female pheasant, is plain brown so she cannot be seen by enemies as she sits on her eggs. Pheasant chicks can run almost as soon as they hatch.

male pheasant

female pheasant

lapwing

lapwing chicks

The lapwing or "peewit" makes its nest on the ground, hiding the eggs and young in a clump of grass.

Birds of the Town

kestrel

A kestrel hovers in the air, ready to swoop on a sparrow.

pied wagtail

sparrows

House sparrows live in all parts of a city.

The pied wagtail nests where warm air comes from a building.

house martin

The house martin builds its mud nest under a ledge.

house martin

Pigeons often nest on window ledges in towns.

pigeon

Starlings line up on ledges in city centers to sleep.

starlings

Many birds live among people in cities and towns. There it is easier to find food and to protect themselves from enemies. Some birds, such as starlings and pied wagtails, come to town centers for warmth and shelter. They fly to gardens and parks or even out to the country to feed. Many water birds, especially ducks and gulls, make their homes on park lakes and rivers. Sparrows can live almost anywhere they choose.

To a bird, the buildings in a city or town may look like cliffs or rocky slopes. Birds that can live on cliffs or in rocky places can also live in towns. Pigeons and kestrels nest on rock ledges in the wild and on window ledges in towns.

tufted duck

mandarin duck

black-headed gulls

moorhen

A male pigeon strutting to show off to the female is a common sight in towns.

male pigeon

female pigeon

Many city birds come to bird tables in gardens to find food. Some are fed by people in city parks and squares. In some countries, tits often steal food by perching on milk bottles and pecking through the top to get at the cream inside. Some tits even follow milkmen as they go on their rounds.

blue tit

white stork

In some countries in Europe, white storks build great nests of sticks and twigs on chimney tops. Some people think that storks bring good luck. They build platforms on their roofs so that storks will nest there every year.

Small birds, especially swallows and swifts, often make their nests on buildings. But sometimes the bird's choice of a nesting spot may seem very strange to us. This pied wagtail has built a nest in the rear light of a car in a junkyard.

pied wagtail

Birds sometimes come to towns to sleep because it is warmer there than in the country. Also, they may be safer from enemies in a town. Chimney swifts come to towns to sleep in old factory chimneys. At dusk, a flock of swifts gathers above a chimney. The birds fly in a circle, entering the chimney one by one as night falls. They cling to the walls inside the chimney to sleep. Chimney swifts also build their nests in old chimneys.

chimney swifts

17

Eagles build their nests, called eyries, on rock ledges in high mountains or on top of cliffs.

young eagles

A golden eagle swoops toward the ground, its talons spread, ready to seize its victim.

golden eagle

hood

falcon

HUNTING FOR MAN
For several thousand years, falconers have trained birds of prey to hunt for them as a sport. The bird perches on the falconer's wrist. A hood is placed over its head until it is ready to be released. Then the bird flies off to catch its prey and bring it back to the falconer.

Birds of Prey

Many birds feed on seeds, berries or other fruit. Others eat insects, and some hunt even larger creatures. They prey upon other birds, rabbits, mice and other rodents, and even fish. These hunting birds include cranes, owls and kingfishers, and a special group of birds called birds of prey.

The birds of prey all have sharp talons for gripping and hooked beaks for tearing flesh. Some, like the great eagles, soar high in the sky, using their sharp eyes to spot their prey on the ground below. They swoop down to the ground to pounce on their victims. Eagles are strong enough to seize animals as large as a lamb or a young deer.

This peregrine falcon has killed a pigeon in the air with a slash of its sharp talons.

peregrine falcon

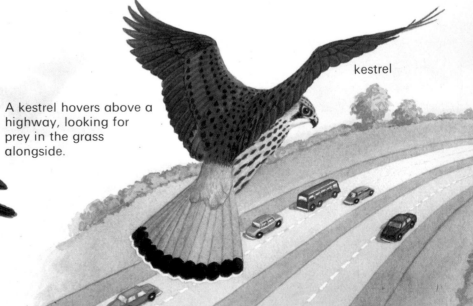

A kestrel hovers above a highway, looking for prey in the grass alongside.

kestrel

The red kite soars through the air, keeping a sharp eye on the ground below. It can spot small animals from a great height.

red kite

The osprey dives "feet first" in or onto the water to "spear" a fish with its sharp talons. It carries off its prey to a tree or cliff to eat it.

A secretary bird will kill and swallow snakes over 3 feet (1 meter) long.

osprey

A white-headed vulture circles over a dead zebra. Vultures feed on the flesh of dead animals, called "carrion."

secretary bird

white-headed vulture

penguin

emu

Flightless Birds

Some birds cannot fly. Their wings are small and useless. Ostriches and emus are flightless birds. They escape danger by running very fast. Penguins use their wings, but only as paddles in the water. The kiwi of New Zealand hides in a burrow during the day and hunts at night. Its tiny wings are hidden beneath hair-like feathers.

kiwi

Millions of passenger pigeons lived in North America only a hundred years ago. Men killed the birds by hunting them and destroying their forests, and by 1915 they were extinct.

Vanishing Birds

Some birds have disappeared from the Earth. Because men hunted them, they became rarer and rarer until the last one died. They are now extinct. The dodo was a large, flightless bird that lived on an island in the Indian Ocean. It was hunted by sailors for food. The dodo has been extinct for over 300 years.

dodo

passenger pigeon

Tropical Forests

In the forests of the hot parts of the world, tree trunks rise like columns to a leafy roof high above. Many beautiful and brightly colored birds live in these forests. Most live in the tops of the trees, feeding on the fruits and flowers there. Other birds fly between the tree trunks, catching insects in the air. On the ground, birds such as pheasants search for food in the undergrowth.

Tropical birds make beautiful and intelligent pets. Many people enjoy keeping parrots, macaws, parakeets, cockatoos, and budgerigars. Some of these birds like to copy the sounds they hear. They can be taught to "talk," though they do not understand what they are saying.

harpy eagle

monkeys

The harpy eagle flies through the tops of the trees, swooping down to seize monkeys and birds in its strong claws.

toucan

The toucan uses its huge beak to reach between the branches and pick fruit.

Hummingbirds hover in the air, dipping their long beaks into flowers to feed on nectar. Their wings move much more quickly than those of most other birds.

macaw

quetzal

The quetzal flutters from one perch to another, trailing its long green feathers. It eats insects and fruit from the trees.

The macaw is a kind of parrot. It uses its claws to hold a nut. Then it cracks the nut open with its beak.

hummingbirds

Sunbirds show off their brilliant colors as they take nectar from the flowers.

sunbirds

The male hornbill seals the female inside a hole in a tree so that she can nest in safety. He leaves a small hole through which he can pass her food.

male hornbill

female bird of paradise

male bird of paradise

Birds of paradise are among the most beautiful birds of the tropical forest. Only the male bird is brightly colored. He attracts the female with his bright feathers and they mate. The female looks after the eggs and young. Her dull plumage hides her from enemies.

The male lyrebird raises a beautiful fan of plumes to attract a female.

lyrebird

The cassowary cannot fly. But it can move quickly through the undergrowth, pushing aside the branches with its bony head.

The pitta spends most of its time on the forest floor, feeding on insects and other small ground creatures. It sleeps in the trees for safety.

cassowary

pitta

Gannets nest in huge colonies on sea cliffs. The young birds are covered with white down at first. Gannets fish by diving straight into the sea from the air.

gannet

young gannet

razorbill

Razorbills are expert divers and can chase fish under water. They nest in colonies on cliffs during the spring and summer, and spend the winter at sea.

Kittiwakes are a type of seagull, but they fly much farther out to sea than other gulls. They scoop up most of their food from the surface of the water.

kittiwake

kittiwake

A guillemot's egg is pear-shaped, which stops it rolling off the edge of the cliff.

guillemot

guillemot's egg

A puffin can catch several fish and hold them in its mouth to carry to its nest.

Sea and Shore Birds

Many different kinds of birds live near the sea. They may feed on the shore or in the sea itself. Gulls, terns, cormorants, gannets and auks fly over the waves near the shore. Some settle on the water to ride the waves, or duck their heads under the water to catch a fish. Others dive from high in the air and splash into the water.

In spring and summer, many of these fishing birds crowd together on cliff ledges or on rocky islands to nest. In winter, many sea birds travel thousands of miles to warmer parts of the world.

Some sea birds live on beaches or on mud flats where rivers flow into the sea. They feed on shellfish, worms and grubs. Their long legs and beaks help them to wade in shallow water and probe for food in the mud. Other birds scurry over the beach, looking for food in the sand. In spring, many of them fly inland to nest and raise their young on moors and on marshes.

puffin

22

The tern looks a bit like a seagull, except that it has a forked tail. Unlike the gull, which usually settles on the surface of the water to find food, the tern flies low over the sea until it spots a fish. Then it dives into the water to catch it.

tern

albatross

Unlucky Bird

Sailors once believed that the albatross was an unlucky bird that brought storms. This is partly true. The albatross needs wind to fly well, and wind often brings storms.

Pelicans sometimes fish by forming a line and driving the fish into the shore.

pelicans

The avocet lowers its turned-up beak to scoop food from the water.

avocet

dunlins

curlew

Dunlins and curlews like muddy and sandy shores. They probe for food with their long, slender beaks.

The turnstone pushes over pebbles with its beak to find small animals. The oystercatcher can open shellfish with its beak.

cormorant

Fishing for Man

In some parts of the world, people train cormorants to fish for them. Each bird is kept on a long lead, with a ring around its neck to stop it swallowing the fish.

turnstone

oystercatcher

Finding Food

Every bird has a beak that is specially shaped for eating certain foods. The hawfinch has a powerful beak to crack open seeds. The hummingbird's beak is a long, thin tube with which it sucks up nectar. The hedge sparrow, or dunnock, has a sharp beak to catch insects. The darter spears fish with its beak, while the pouched beak of the pelican catches fish like a net. The eagle uses its beak for tearing meat, and the merganser grips fish with its saw-like beak. The scoop-like beak of the flamingo strains small creatures from the water.

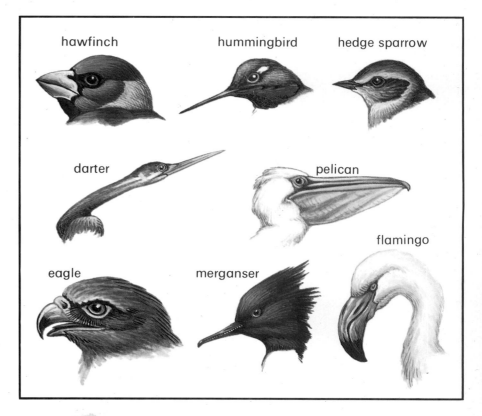

hawfinch hummingbird hedge sparrow

darter pelican

flamingo

eagle merganser

woodpecker finch

The woodpecker finch uses a cactus spine to dig insects out of bark.

Egyptian vulture

The Egyptian vulture drops a stone on an ostrich egg to crack it open.

song thrush

The song thrush hammers a snail onto a stone to break open its shell.

pigeon

sparrow

Like most birds, the sparrow has to tip its head back to swallow water. But the pigeon can drink by sucking up water.

Some birds use a tool to get at their food, as shown in the pictures at the left. Other birds eat food that is provided by man. Gulls follow plows and gobble up worms as the soil is turned (below). They also follow ships and pick up any food that is thrown into the sea.

gulls plow

Keeping Clean

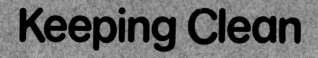
chaffinches

A bird has thousands of feathers to keep clean. Each day the feathers gather dirt and pests such as fleas and lice. Also, the feathers become ragged. To clean and tidy themselves, birds often run their beaks through their feathers. This action is called preening. Some birds preen each other.

Chaffinches preen each other with their beaks.

chaffinches

A dipper rubs its beak against its oil gland before oiling its feathers. Water birds need plenty of oil to stop their feathers getting too wet and heavy.

dipper

Taking a bath also helps to clean the feathers. Most birds take a dip in water when they find it, fluttering their wings to splash themselves. Some birds oil their feathers as well. They use their beaks to take oil from a special gland near the tail. They spread this oil over their feathers. The oil helps to make the feathers waterproof.

A bird cannot use its beak to clean its head. Instead it scratches its head with a claw. Even with good cleaning, the feathers do not last for ever. New ones grow every year, though not all at once.

Sparrows bathe by splashing in water or by taking a dust bath.

sparrows

A starling places ants among its feathers. The ants help to clean the starling by eating tiny insect pests.

heron

starling

greenfinches

goldfinch

A heron scratches its plumage with a claw to remove some muddy slime. Some of its feathers make a special powder that helps dry the slime before the heron scratches it off.

Bird Defense

Most birds have enemies. Cats, rats and foxes catch birds on the ground or raid nests for eggs and young birds. Even in the air, birds are not safe. Birds of prey chase and catch them in flight.

All birds have ways of escaping danger. Some only come out at night, when they cannot be spotted easily. But most birds are out in the daytime, when they are feeding. Many of them have feathers that are specially colored to match their surroundings. This is called camouflage. It makes the birds very difficult for their enemies to see.

nightjar

woodcock

The colors of the nightjar help to hide it among bracken, dead leaves and wood.

The snowy owl and the ptarmigan live in cold places where snow covers the ground in winter. Their white feathers make them difficult to see in the snow.

The woodcock makes a nest in a shallow dip in the ground. After lining the nest with leaves, she lays three or four eggs that are well camouflaged against the leafy nest.

garden warbler

The Hidden Singer
The garden warbler, like many songbirds, has colors that hide it among the leaves of a tree or bush. It can sing loudly without giving away its position.

snowy owl

ptarmigan

Some birds cannot fly, but they have long and powerful legs and can run very fast to escape their enemies. When nests are in danger, parent birds may try to drive intruders away. The birds fly at their enemies in an action called "mobbing" to try to scare them off. They may even strike them to stop them getting to the eggs or young.

common terns

Common terns mob a birdwatcher who is too close to their nests.

ostrich

An ostrich runs from a lion. Ostriches can reach speeds of up to 40 mph (65 km/hr).

lion

Plovers protect their nests by pretending to be hurt. When an enemy such as a fox approaches the nest, the parent bird calls out and runs along the ground, dragging one wing as if it is broken. The fox follows the parent bird, because it looks easy to catch. When the plover has led the fox far from the nest, it stops pretending and flies away. Plovers sometimes play this trick on people near their nests.

fox

A killdeer, a kind of plover, leads a fox away from the eggs in its nest by pretending to be injured.

killdeer nest

killdeer

Feeding Birds

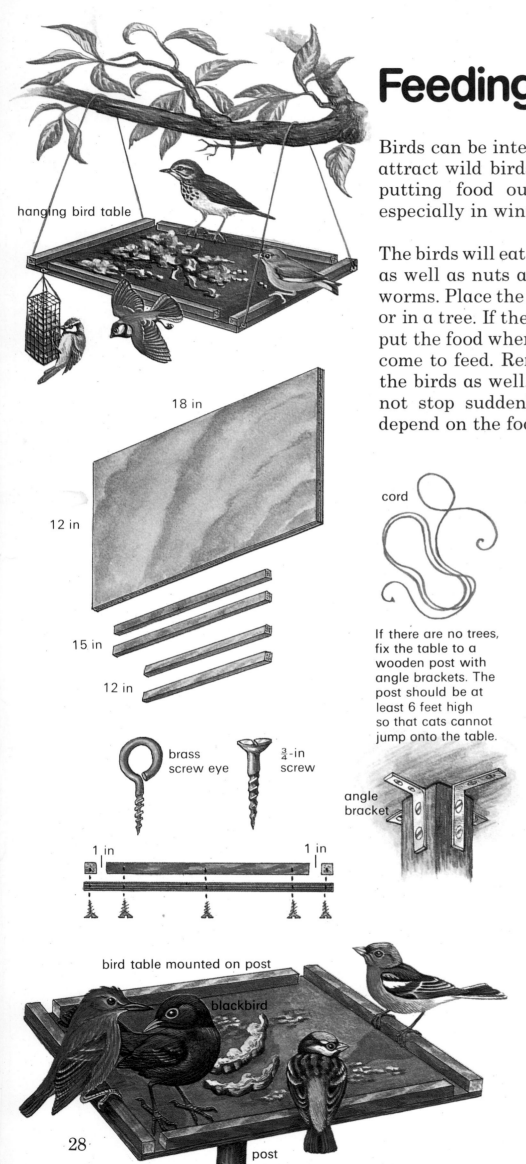

hanging bird table

18 in

12 in

15 in

12 in

cord

If there are no trees, fix the table to a wooden post with angle brackets. The post should be at least 6 feet high so that cats cannot jump onto the table.

brass screw eye

¾-in screw

angle bracket

1 in   1 in

bird table mounted on post

blackbird

28

post

Birds can be interesting and fun to watch. You can attract wild birds to your garden or windowsill by putting food out for them. They will like this especially in winter, when food is hard to find.

The birds will eat almost any scraps from the kitchen as well as nuts and fruit. Insect eaters enjoy small worms. Place the food on a bird table or a windowsill or in a tree. If there are cats and dogs around, try to put the food where they cannot get at the birds that come to feed. Remember to put out some water for the birds as well. If you do feed birds in winter, do not stop suddenly. The birds may have come to depend on the food you give them.

Making a bird table

A bird table is simply a flat tray fastened to the top of a post, hung from a tree, or placed outside a window. A good bird table can be made cheaply and simply. This is how to do it.

You will need a piece of marine plywood, which resists rain, $\frac{1}{2}$ in thick and measuring 12 in by 18 in; a strip of wood $\frac{1}{2}$ in by $\frac{1}{2}$ in and 54 in long; and a dozen $\frac{3}{4}$-in brass screws or galvanized nails. Cut the strip into two 15-in and two 12-in lengths, and fix them along the top edges of the plywood, leaving a 1-in gap at each corner. Do this by screwing or nailing from below through the plywood first to prevent the plywood splitting. Coat the wood with a wood preservative to make it last a long time.

To hang the table, insert a brass or galvanized screw eye at each corner. Loop two lengths of nylon cord over the branch of a tree and tie the ends to the screw eyes.

Hanging food

Birds often enjoy food if you hang it up for them. They can land on the food and peck at it as it swings to and fro. Some small birds are very good at this. Sparrows find it a bit more difficult, but they may try, too.

The food can be hung on a piece of string or placed in a food basket. The plastic netting in which lemons and onions are often wrapped is useful for making a food basket. Pet shops also sell net bags of nuts. Never hang out salted nuts, because they will harm the birds.

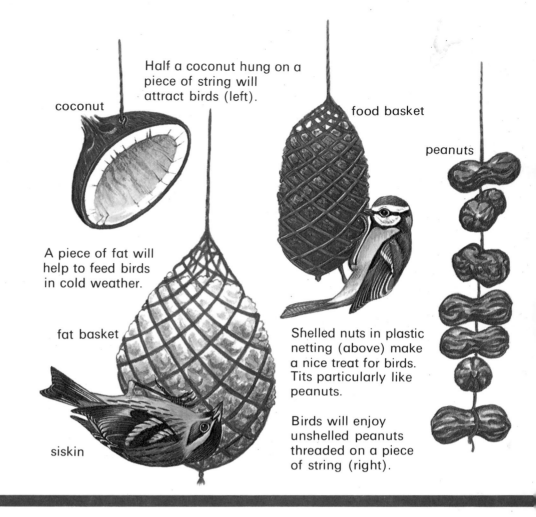

coconut

Half a coconut hung on a piece of string will attract birds (left).

food basket

peanuts

A piece of fat will help to feed birds in cold weather.

fat basket

siskin

Shelled nuts in plastic netting (above) make a nice treat for birds. Tits particularly like peanuts.

Birds will enjoy unshelled peanuts threaded on a piece of string (right).

Index